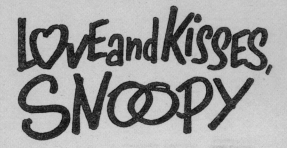

Love and Kisses, SNOOPY

Selected Cartoons from

SUMMERS FLY, WINTERS WALK

Vol. 2

by CHARLES M. SCHULZ

FAWCETT CREST • NEW YORK

LOVE AND KISSES, SNOOPY

This book prepared especially for Fawcett Crest Books, a unit of CBS Publications, the Consumer Publishing division of CBS Inc., comprises a portion of SUMMERS FLY, WINTERS WALK and is reprinted by arrangement with Holt, Rinehart and Winston, Inc.

Contents of Book: PEANUTS® comic strips by Charles M. Schulz. Copyright © 1976 by United Feature Syndicate, Inc.

ISBN: 0-449-24292-7

Printed in the United States of America

First Fawcett Crest printing: May 1980

10 9 8 7 6 5 4 3 2 1

LOVE and KISSES, SNOOPY

Dear Pen Pal,
It has been a long time since I have written to you.
Things are pretty much the same around here
Especially my penmanship.
SCHULZ

Dear Pen Pal,
Today I am going to try to write you a neat letter.
No smudges and no smears
LOOK AT THAT! YOU SMEARED "SMUDGE," AND YOU SMUDGED "SMEAR"! THAT'S VERY FUNNY! DON'T YOU THINK THAT'S FUNNY?
I THOUGHT IT WAS VERY FUNNY!

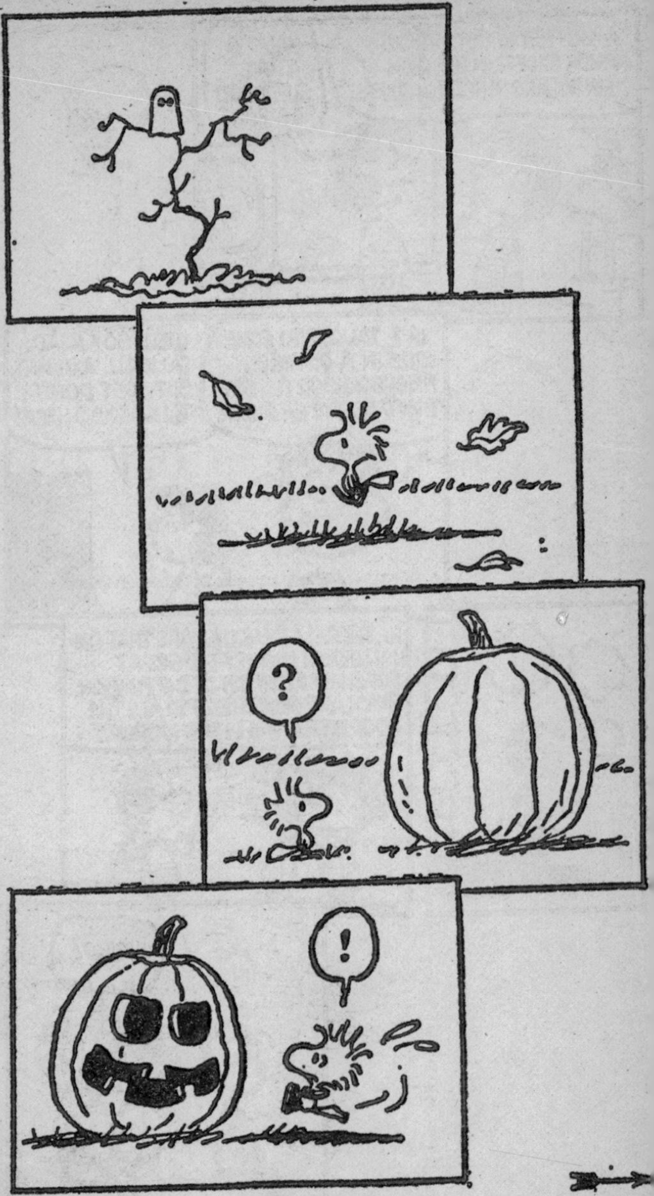

PEANUTS

YOU'RE A PAL, SNOOPY!
(selected cartoons from
You Need Help Charlie Brown, Vol. 2)   23775-3 $1.25

PLAY BALL, SNOOPY
(selected cartoons from
Win a Few, Lose a Few, Charlie Brown, Vol. 1)
                                                23222-0 $1.25

YOU'VE GOT TO BE KIDDING, SNOOPY!
(selected cartoons from
Speak Softly and Carry a Beagle, Vol. 1)   23453-3 $1.25

HERE'S TO YOU, CHARLIE BROWN
(selected cartoons from
You Can't Win, Charlie Brown, Vol. 2)   23708-7 $1.25

HEY, PEANUTS!
(selected cartoons from
More Peanuts, Vol. II)   24013-4 $1.25

                                                          8006

This offer expires 1/28/81